the lettering book
COMPANION

 Noelene Morris   Audra Ninowski

Audra Ninowski's

Book

AN ASHTON ORIGINAL

from Ashton Scholastic
Sydney Auckland New York Toronto London

To Zora

National Library of Australia
Cataloguing-in-Publication data

Morris, Noelene.
   The lettering book companion.

   ISBN 0 86896 131 6.

   1. Lettering — Juvenile literature. 2. Borders Ornamental
   (Decorative arts) — Juvenile literature.
   I. Title.

   745.6′1

First published in 1987 by Ashton Scholastic Pty Limited (Inc. in NSW),
PO Box 579, Gosford 2250. Also in Brisbane, Melbourne, Adelaide, Perth
and Auckland, NZ.

Typeset by Veritage Press Pty Ltd, Gosford NSW.
Printed by Tien Wah Press (Pte) Limited.

12 11 10 9 8 7 6 5 4 3 2 1   6 7 8 9 / 8 0 1 / 9

CONTENTS

About this Book

Following the great success of *The Lettering Book* my students and colleagues asked me for a book of borders which they could use to enhance their lettering.

The Lettering Book Companion contains a multitude of border styles as well as a variety of decorative symbols and markers. Many are quite simple to draw and, although others are more elaborate, they should all inspire you to experiment.

With *The Lettering Book Companion* you no longer have to be artistically talented to present your work effectively. I hope you have fun deciding which borders to use and that this book increases your confidence when preparing any written work. Good luck and happy drawing!

Presentation and Design

Effective presentation of written work relies on more than attractive lettering.

A continuous slab of written material is boring to the reader and, if being presented for assessment, is probably less likely to earn good marks.

Highlight your introductions or summaries by placing them within a border. Emphasise important points in this way too. When using a number of borders together it is best to use simple designs which complement one another.

Decorative marks or symbols can be used to break up lengthy text and to emphasise important points.
- Use them to distinguish one fact from another and allow a little spacing around each point.
- Symbols are very effective in posters and are frequently seen in advertising.
- Businesses often use a symbol or logo as a trademark.

There are many decorative and stylish borders which can enhance your work visually. Yet a single curved line or simple ruled lines, used sparingly, will complete your efforts with distinction.

The presentation of written work is usually as important as its content. Spend a few minutes on preparation and you can turn a plain page into an eye-catching masterpiece. With practice, you should become skilled in the use of a variety of borders, symbols and rules in conjunction with your lettering styles.

Tips for Better Borders

- Start with simple designs — simple borders are often more effective than fancy ones.

- Choose designs you like to draw.

- Select a design which suits your subject.

- Consider the time you have available — some borders and printing styles take much longer than others to draw.

- Don't clutter your page — spacing is important.

- It's important to plan and sketch your page first. Then you can step back and judge spacing and effect.

- It's best to sketch guidelines in a soft lead pencil (2B) which can be erased easily.

- Use a ruler for all straight lines and a set square for all right-angled corners.

- There are lots of drawing materials on the market so use the pens or pencils that give the effect you like.

- Limit the number of colours you use for borders and titles, otherwise you will spoil the visual effect.

Border Designs

Some designs have straight or square corners.

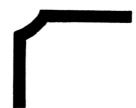

Some lines are thick.

Some designs have curved or rounded corners.

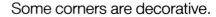

Some lines are thin.

Some corners are decorative.

Some designs are shaded or coloured.

Some borders are imaginative.

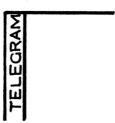

TELEGRAM

Some patterns continue around the whole border.

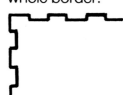

Making Great Borders

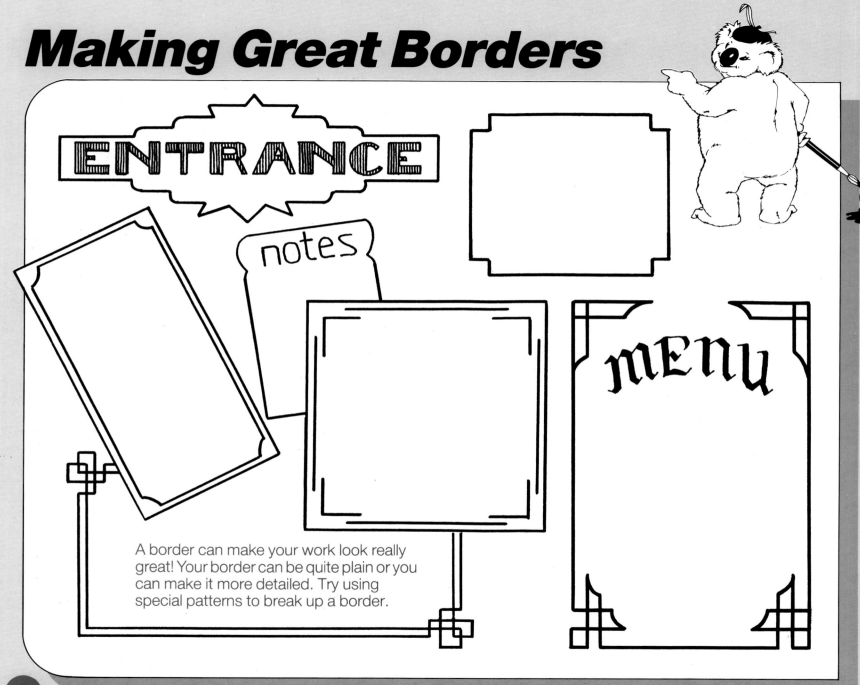

ENTRANCE

notes

MENU

A border can make your work look really great! Your border can be quite plain or you can make it more detailed. Try using special patterns to break up a border.

NOW SHOWING

review

You can find new ideas for borders everywhere!

9

More Great Borders

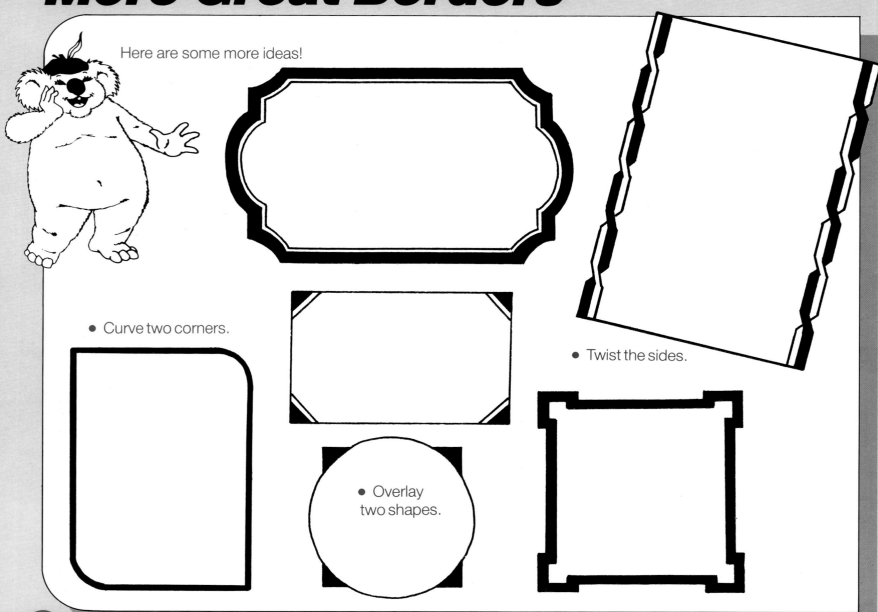

Here are some more ideas!

- Curve two corners.

- Twist the sides.

- Overlay two shapes.

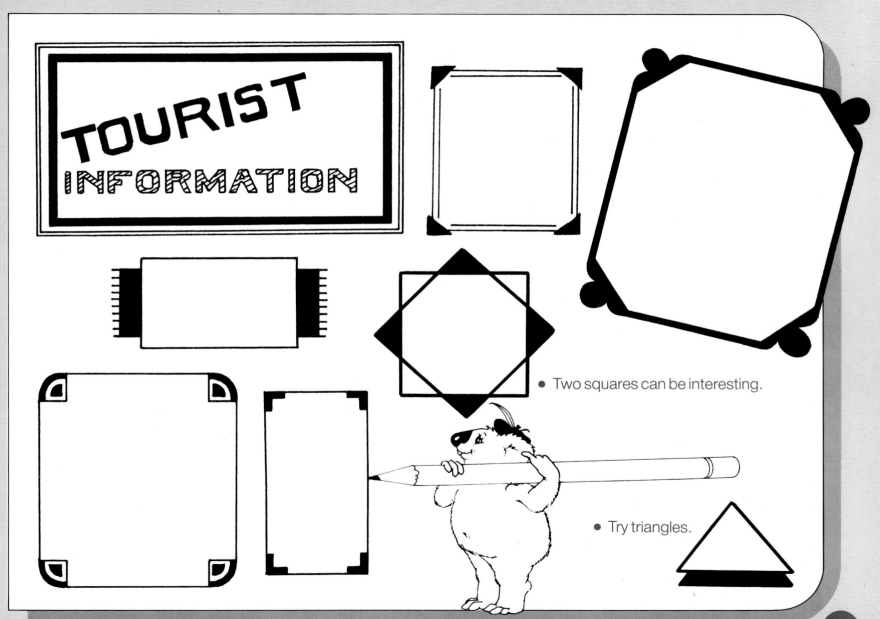

TOURIST INFORMATION

- Two squares can be interesting.

- Try triangles.

Broken Borders

Borders are not just solid lines. You can make them up from little lines and patterns.

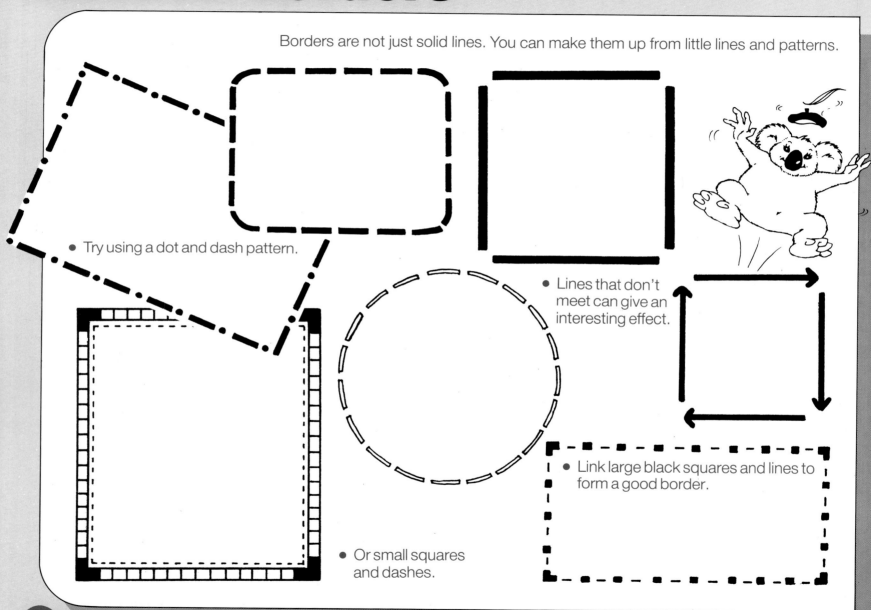

- Try using a dot and dash pattern.

- Lines that don't meet can give an interesting effect.

- Link large black squares and lines to form a good border.

- Or small squares and dashes.

MY FAMILY

- Even more complex broken patterns are good.

13

Wide Borders

You can make a border really bold by widening it.

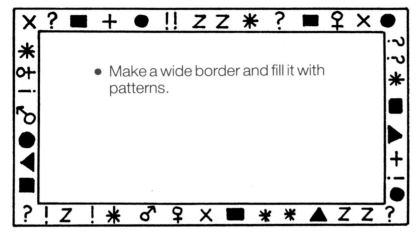

- Make a wide border and fill it with patterns.

- Try making one or two sides wider than the others.

CONTENTS

REPORT

- Make variations on an ordinary shape.

- Curve the corners.

Changing Sides

Make up new patterns for the sides of borders to create unusual effects.

LIBRA

- Change the shape of just one side.

LINES

- Add a shadow to a border to make it more striking.

- Carve out a border from a different shape.

- Try a pattern on two sides.

ENTRANCE

EXIT

Pets

Cutting Corners

Interesting effects can be achieved by changing the corners.

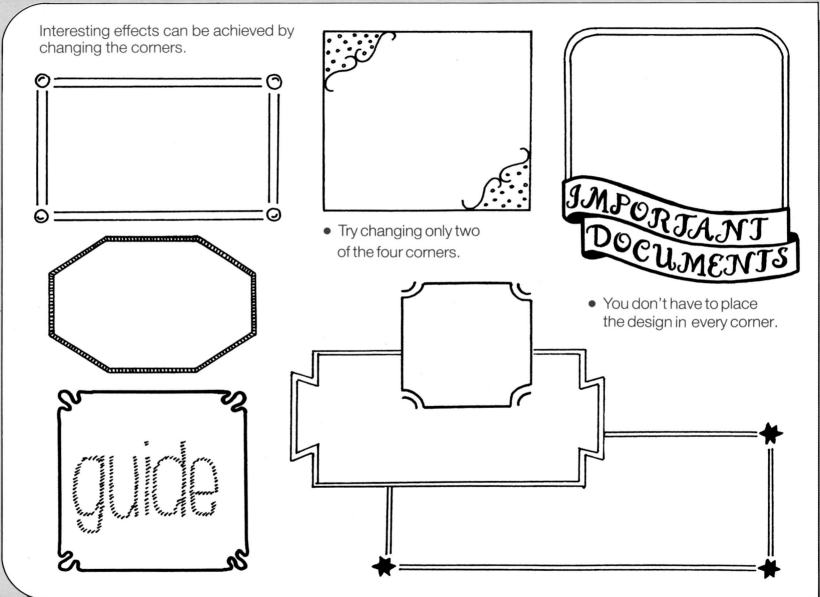

- Try changing only two of the four corners.

- You don't have to place the design in every corner.

IMPORTANT DOCUMENTS

guide

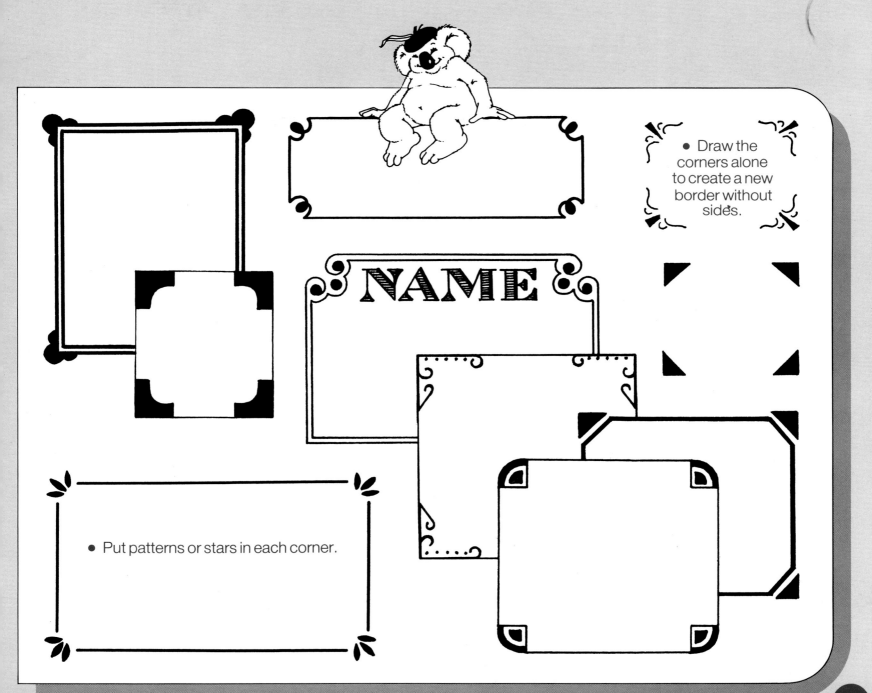

NAME

- Draw the corners alone to create a new border without sides.

- Put patterns or stars in each corner.

Unusual Borders

• Try a curved pattern.

• Try curving a plain border.

Borders don't have to be straight lines.

splot

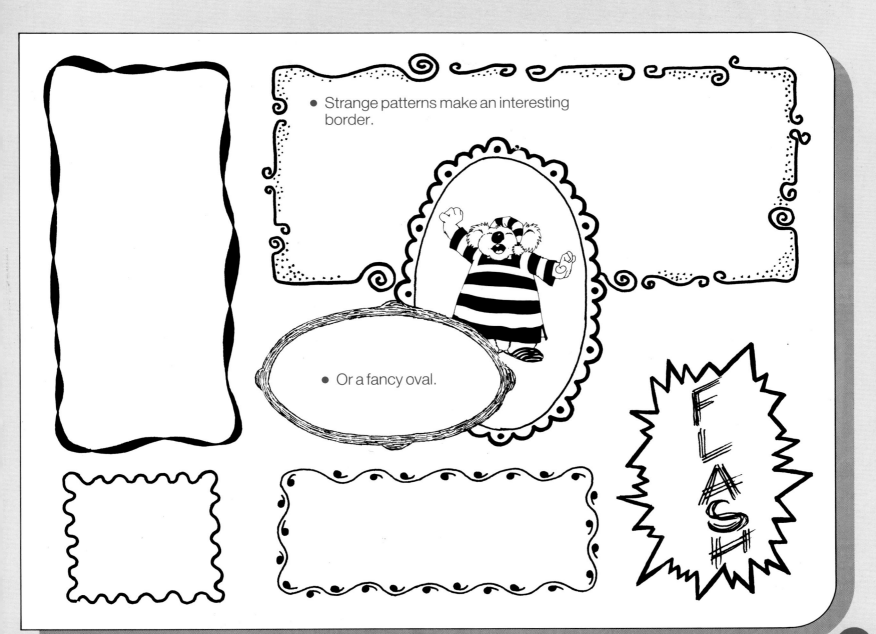

• Strange patterns make an interesting border.

• Or a fancy oval.

Interesting Shapes

Try getting adventurous with your border designs.

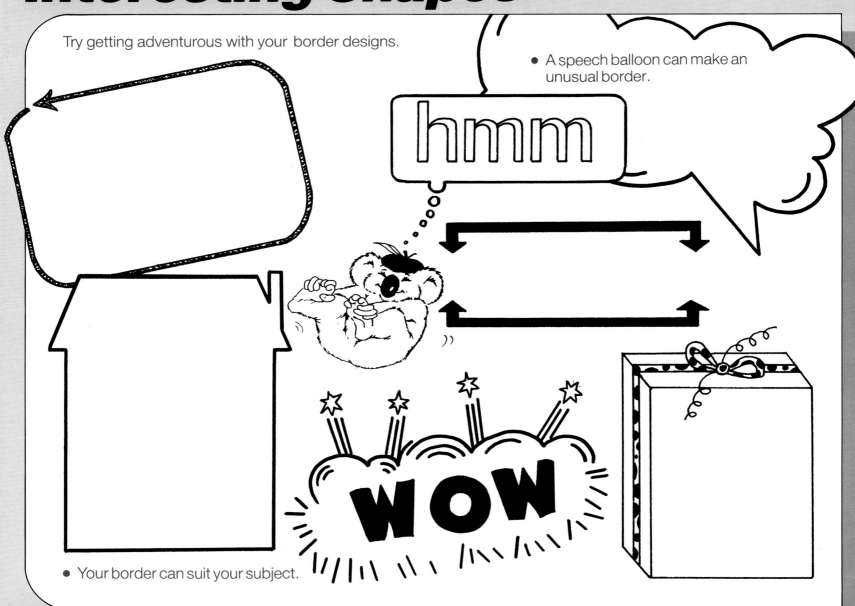

- A speech balloon can make an unusual border.

hmm

- Your border can suit your subject.

WOW

Topical Borders

Design a border to suit your topic. Try using words or symbols to suit the theme of your work.

FIRE

chocolate wheel — drinks — tea — fun — rides — stalls — ghost house — art display — dogs — plants

Best Wishes

SHIPS

ON THE FARM

PLANTS

meat meat meat meat meat meat meat meat

FOR SALE

SCIENCE • SCIENCE • SCIENCE • SCIENCE • SCIENCE

Pictures or Borders?

Your lettering can become a whole picture with the right border.

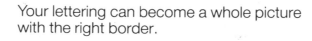

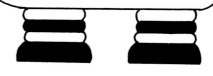

Decorations and Arrows

Try using arrows or decorative symbols to break up large slabs of text, or to list important points.

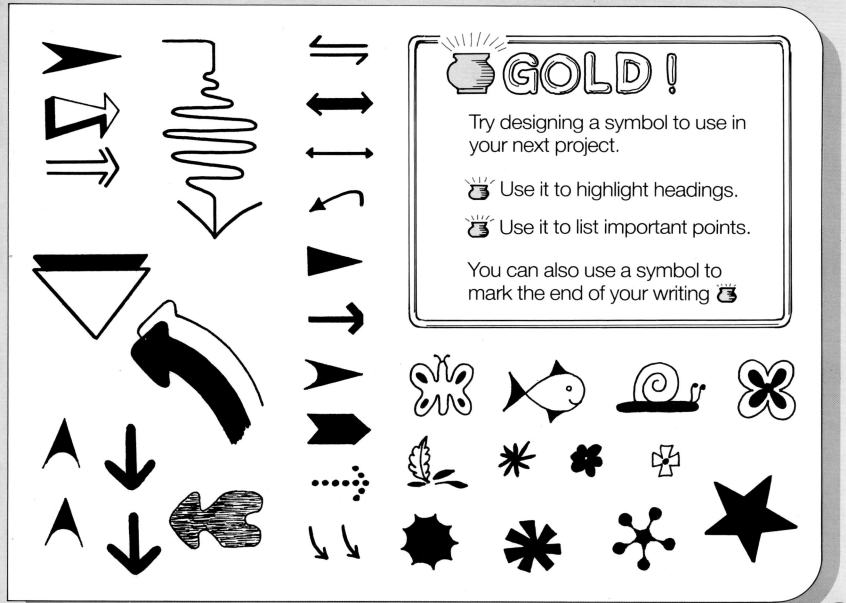

GOLD!

Try designing a symbol to use in your next project.

- Use it to highlight headings.

- Use it to list important points.

You can also use a symbol to mark the end of your writing

29

Scrolls

Scrolls add interest. They are best used to highlight headings.

EXPLORATION

ANNIVERSARY

WORKBOOK

GOLD

TIMETABLE

HISTORY

Headings

Headings are very important. Choose a lettering style which suits the subject. Try to make all headings eye-catching.

Clipboards and Boxes

Our Holiday

gift...

INDEX

PARTY